Digital Marketing Practice Guide for SMBs

(SEO,SEM and SMM Practice Guide)

By

Venkataramana Rolla

Table of Contents

Chapter 10 – Digital Marketing Step by Step

- **Some Technical Tips**

Introduction

SEO is currently very much essential for the small and medium businesses and especially for the online businesses. Here, many of these small and medium businesses are finding it difficult to hire a professional for their SEO needs. This practice guide is designed in a way every business owner can practice SEO on own with little patience, little time and increased confidence. In fact, SEO is not a difficult aspect as long as you can acquaint a little about the search engines, their working and search engine algorithm. This practice guide is going to offer ample awareness, idea and familiarity with these aspects in a way practicing SEO can be easy for all. There is no necessity to have some technical or IT background to work on your SEO needs. Just follow the way things mentioned in this guide and allow the things fall into the places effortlessly for you and for your website.

SEO or search engine optimization is definitely not a technical process as long as one can have a practical approach. It is all about finding out, how a search engine working for the users and plan some strategies basing on it for your website SEO. The entire SEO practice is separated with special chapters and sub chapters in a way the user can practice SEO very easily. Current day digital marketing world is definitely brimming with the huge competition and this competition is very easy to overcome using some of the best techniques in the search engine optimization. Personally, I am a freelance writer and working for many clients all over the world on their SEO needs. My exposure and experiences in this field through serving well to the worldwide clientele motivated me to write this practice guide with more practical and positive approach. Hope this guide can be of help for your needs more effectively.

Chapter 1: SEO Basics with Digital Marketing Perspective

Digital Marketing

This digital marketing world is currently spread all over the internet and serving well to the worldwide customer base successfully too. Current day customer base is more into the virtual world for their shopping needs over the physical markets. This kind of trend is growing significantly all over the world due to the involved convenience and economy for the shopping. Also, this kind of online shopping model, which is called as digital marketing world is nowadays occupied maximum share of the worldwide markets too. Mainly, this online marketing using a website is nowadays more cost effective business model for the current day entrepreneurs and most of the entrepreneurs are making good use of this business model to a great extent. Actually, this kind of increased interest towards the digital marketing world from everyone in this world is creating the huge competition for every business product or service online.

Digital marketing arena over the internet is currently facing huge competition through having the lakhs of websites those are selling similar product or service online. It is clearly indicating that every product or service online nowadays is facing competition from thousand to lakhs in the form of the various websites and blogs. Here, SEO is going to play a vital role to combat well against this huge competition. Websites those are selling similar product or service online proving their competitiveness successfully through applying the wise SEO strategies. If any online business wanted to do well online, then it is highly imperative to have special SEO strategies without fail. Your search engine optimization strategies in the right form can keep you as a great contender and competitor at business front with all your competitors successfully.

Definitely, digital marketing world is enormous keeping in mind the presence of the billions of entrepreneurs online with the business products and services. Here, every upcoming and current digital format business model should have proper planning, approach and practice for the search engine optimization without fail.

Practicing SEO for your online business is going to be little time taking task initially, but turns into simple, easy and quicker for you down the line. This kind of own practice will turn you into a perfect professionally instantly and saves a lot of money from hiring a professional too. My further chapters are going to offer in detail idea and right approach for this purpose.

Internet Marketing

Internet marketing is nothing, but a strategy that is to improve the sales and business online with appropriate techniques. When you have a website and selling multiple products online through this website, then proper internet marketing approach should be bundled with the business without fail. This internet marketing is all about projecting your product(s) or service(s) well to the customer base online with right and promising approaches. There are so many methods available for this internet marketing, but SEO always works into a basic back bone for the internet marketing strategy. It is clearly indicating that the search engine optimization is always a major necessity for the every online business to excel well over the internet. Here, this kind of optimization is always a best approach towards attracting the organic traffic towards your website. Organic traffic that is generated through a popular search engine such as Google can result into the huge business for the present and future too.

Internet marketing can be practiced in multiple ways successfully, but most of these aspects will look like pure marketing strategies and some will fail drastically too. Here, practicing some of the right optimization techniques for the internet marketing is always a great help for the business sustenance and future growth in many ways. This is the reason, I am not going to tell further more about other internet marketing types as I have planned this guide more SEO, SEM and SMM centric. Definitely, search engine optimization is one of the promising approaches for the successful internet marketing needs. Mainly, the traffic obtained through the search engines and search engine page rankings will improve the reliability for your business to a good extent. It is always a well known fact that a business that is reliable with the customer base will live forever successfully. This similar strategy will work well for the online business too and obtain this reliability successfully and quickly using some of the best and reliable SEO, SEM and SMM techniques.

Internet marketing using search engine optimization is always better approach for the current day small and medium businesses. Many of the present day successful online small and medium businesses successfully gained a lot through this approach. This is the reason, why I planned to present this guide to the SMEs those are finding it tough to afford right SEO/SEM/SMM for their business websites. Small and medium businesses are always established keeping in mind that it requires very little investment. Here, these entrepreneurs always find it difficult to hire a professional for the SEO needs. Also, it is highly essential and good to have dynamic SEO approach for the online business too. Hiring a professional for this purpose for a long term is highly tough for the present day small and medium online businesses. Such businesses can successfully make good use of my guide to a great extent.

Search Engines and Their Working

Search engines are currently helping a lot for everyone in this world for their special needs online besides helping a lot for their shopping needs in addition. Here, it is quite imperative to understand more about these search engines and popular search engines online.

Popular Search Engines:

1. Google
2. Bing
3. Yahoo
4. Lycos
5. Babylon
6. Baidu (Chinese search engine)
7. Yandex (Russian search engine)

Currently, Google is leading ahead over all other popular search engines in the world with a lion share in the worldwide search engine markets. According to the reports, Google is currently occupied around 44% of the worldwide search engine market. So, it is always good to plan your website optimization keeping in mind Google in a way to be in reach for the maximum customer base in the world. Also, you need not have to restrict your optimization only for the Google and extend it further with other search engines too with simple steps those will be explained well in the further chapters for you.

Google search technology is currently very strong unlike earlier. Earlier, their search algorithm used to offer results with some flaws. Now, it is not the case and their algorithm is completely strong in a way to match well to their strategies. Google algorithm works little different from other search engine algorithms as an effort to offer the useful and valuable information for the search engine users. Here, their algorithm is designed in a way to provide the more reliable results those are very much apt for the users' requirements. Google prioritizes their search engine results page basing up on the authority. It will identify some of the authority sites to list in the top for every search query. Here, this kind of special strategy is arrived to provide the genuine and reliable information for the user.

For example, you're searching for a health related issues online using Google search engine. The results will arrive in a routine format to inform you that the Google has identified some of the authority sites for this query and those will be displayed without fail within the top 1 to 6 results. As you searched for the health related topic, Google will provide you very often the www.webmd.com site definitely within the top three results. It is a well known fact that this particular site is very much genuine and offer the fair information on any kind f health related topic. Similarly, the rest results will be credited with the Wikipedia, YouTube video, latest news etc. So, every time, the top results will be with one authority site, Wikipedia, news site and video. Here, this example is furnished keeping in mind to offer you a clear idea about, how the Google search engine works for a user. Here, it is quite imperative to understand this strategy, which can offer you a great deal of awareness over the Google search engine algorithm to a great extent too. This is the way you have to understand about other search engines working too through verifying the results with various search queries. When you planned to practice SEO on own, then it is essential to understand the working of the search engine first.

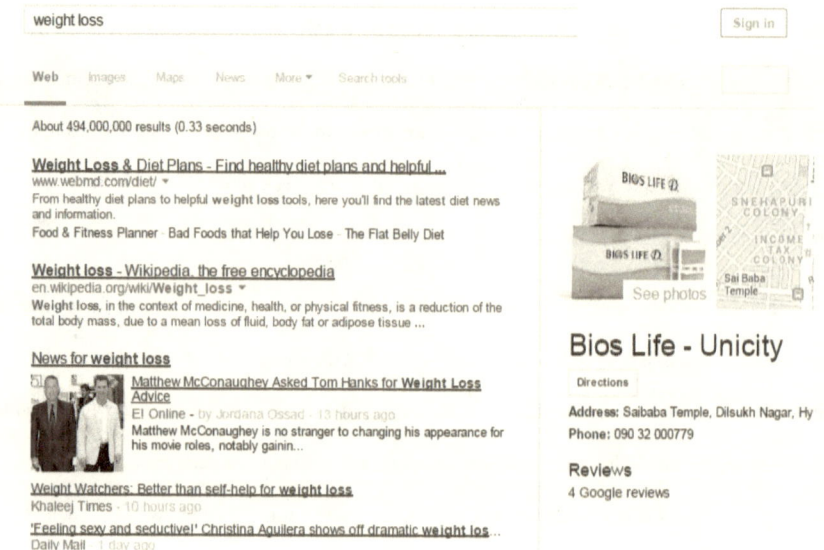

The above image is clearly showing you the SERP that is for "weight loss" query. You can see the first result as www.webmd.com, second result as Wikipedia and third from the latest news site. This is the way generally to results will be given to authority sites by the Google that can be seen with regularly Wikipedia, YouTube videos and some more very regularly.

As I mentioned earlier, Google already occupied the lion share in the search market and let us plan our search engine optimization practice guide for the Google. It is highly imperative to have a great idea on the resulting Search Engine page Results (SERP) with Google in the above mentioned perspective without fail. It will offer you the exact way of the Google algorithm working for you in detail.

Google Algorithm Updates

Google updates their algorithm at regular intervals keeping in mind the latest trends, user base interests and prevailing practices from the users for SEO, which includes black hat and white hat techniques. Here, Google always tends to upgrade their algorithm in a way the results can be more user friendly besides being capable enough to control the black hat techniques used by the users for their SEO improvements too. These updates are generally come in the form of Google Panda and Google Penguin updates. The latest updates were implemented by Google sometime in the year 2011 and latest updates yet to come from the Google.

Google Panda update is all about the content regulations and Google Penguin update is all about inbound and outbound links clarity and consideration. I hope you all are aware of the latest Penguin update in the Year 2011, which created a great impact on many SMBs those succeeded well through the BuildMyRank services. This update clearly mentioned so many regulations with regards to the inbound links quality and standards. People those obtained good results with the help of 150 words blog posts from the service provider BuildMyRank impacted badly through this update. Most of the websites those belongs to the various SMBs online received notices from the Google asking them to delete all these blog posts, which are totally away from the standards and quality parameters. This incident is clearly indicating to everyone that is into SEO to practice pure white hat techniques without fail.

Google every time comes up with their updates basing up on the trends and practices from the users. So, it is highly essential for you to keep open your SEO strategies in a way to fit well into the current and upcoming algorithm updates without fail. There should be serene and standardized approach without fail for your Search Engine Optimization. I hope this guide will help you to a great extent for this purpose. Mainly, all the SMBs has to keep up their strategy dynamic in a way to stand tall against their competitors those are also into the similar strategy for obtaining business and organic traffic from the Google towards their websites. It is always simple to keep up your approach dynamic all the time successfully using this guide, when failed to hire a professional on constant basis.

Just understand well the Google search architecture and ranking methodology through a pure practical approach and plan a foolproof strategy for your SEO successfully. Here, observing and understanding these aspects is quite simple through the way I mentioned above about the authoritative sites. Just follow the Google guidelines well and come up with the effortless off page optimization to keep up this approach dynamic always.

Yahoo and Bing

Definitely, it is not a good idea to ignore other search engines for your needed organic traffic. My suggestion for this purpose is that SEO keeping in mind Google algorithm and submits your websites to popular search engines' web master tools too without fail. Especially, Bing is currently occupied with the huge volume of mobile searches and do not fail to target this traffic for your website. Just plan the SEO for Google in complete manner following well the guidelines and submit the similar strategy with other search engines too. It may not match well for their algorithm, but stands into a reasonable support for obtaining good traffic from other search engines too.

There is another important aspect I should mention here without fail. Yahoo and Bing are currently sharing the similar search technology through partnering and sharing expenses for the search technology development. So, submitting once your website with yahoo and Bing can bring similar results and similar attention from the users those are into these two search engines. It is worth doing this way and your website will obtain good mileage and benefits from the three search engines at once successfully.

Following links can take you to the right location, where you can submit your website for indexing from the search engines:

1. Google Submission
2. Yahoo Submission
3. Bing Submission
4. Baidu Submission

Chapter 2: Keyword Research and Analysis

Keyword research is always a vital aspect for your SEO. Google AdWords keyword tool is always a great help here for this purpose. I must inform a little about this tool here without fail. Google regularly updates this keyword tool based up on the users and their used search strings within their search engines. This database updates regularly and you can obtain these keywords geographic location wise on monthly basis, daily basis and yearly basis from this tool. It is more trustworthy tool to understand well, how the users are framing their keywords to obtain their results. These keywords will offer you a great level of understanding about the customer base interests and how exactly you can plan your website content in a way to match well with these interests. Also, creating content based up on these keywords can result into the more search engine friendly approach from your side too.

You will be having good volume choices from this keyword tool for your website content. It is always good to select a keyword that is trending at good and matches well to your business product(s) or service(s). Here, some logical approach is very much essential. For example, top trending keyword with users in hundreds of thousands may be a good idea always, but always remember that this type of highly searched keywords is an indication to the huge volume of competition. Generally, top trending keyword with hundreds of thousands searches is an indication that there are thousands of websites already there for this particular keyword. As I mentioned earlier, Google always have a strategy to have authority sites for the top trending keywords from the old, reliable and trustworthy websites. So, there is no point for a new website to go with this top keyword as all your efforts will turn into totally in vain due to the already successful and proved contenders. Here, my suggestion is to go with medium level keyword that is trending with the medium volume of users. This kind of keywords and low trending keywords are always wise approach for a new website SEO strategy.

A new website with medium or low trending keyword will allow you to make mark over the industry. Here, consider this medium or low keyword as your main keyword for the content and select 4 to 5 top trending keywords as your auxiliary keywords. You have to select one main keyword and 4 to 5 auxiliary keywords for creating the each website page content. In this way, you're informing Google that your site is suitable for all these 5 to 6 keyword searches. This kind of approach will offer you a good chance to excel quickly with Google Search Engine page Results. Once after you acquire good web rankings with the medium or low trending keyword, you will stand into an authoritative website for the low or medium keyword. After obtaining this kind of good attention from the search engine, then slowly change your attention to other top trending keywords from bottom to top in a way to reach the top level in a right approach effortlessly. It is a little tricky approach, but works really well for a new website to excel quickly within the web rankings.

You have to conduct some research before selecting the right keyword for your business website. Just verify the each keyword with search engines and find out the keyword that is coming with the less number of authority sites. If you can target the keyword that is with nil or less number of authority sites can help you well to obtain the quick success and authority status for your website. Here, your entire SEO approach should be clean, serene and intertwined with the pure white hat technologies without fail.

You have to conduct competitive analysis for your keyword through searching for the currently trending websites for that particular keyword. Find out the positives and negatives of those websites those are trending well with the search engine with that particular keyword. Here, use all their negatives to your advantage in a way to obtain upper hand over these competitors very easily. This competitive analysis for the keyword with pure practical approach can create a right successful path for your SEO quick success. Here, analysis may sound as a tough word, but it is nothing, but pure observation with the search engine about the status of the every website that is associated with that particular keyword.

Keywords selection is another tricky process here. As I mentioned earlier, you should have one main keyword and 4 to five auxiliary keywords for every page of your website. Select this main keyword basing up on the number of searches taking place every month, but rest keywords should be considered from the keyword tool basing up on the user base interest, their native slang, their colloquial way of language speaking, etc. For example, you're selling flight tickets online. You have to select the auxiliary keywords in multiple formats rather than singular format. Here, idea is that every native speaker will initiate their search for tickets, trains, buses and flights in multiple though they need one for their need. Generally, it is the colloquial way of speaking by native. This way you can target the more volume of the customer base in the right way for your business.

Localized keyword research is always essential, when your business website is serving for a particular location. Google AdWords keyword tool offers the keyword research based on the geographic location. You can use the tool keeping up the location as the entire world or for a particular country or for a particular city or for a particular zip code location successfully. This is the way you can accomplish the localized keyword search for your website too. It is always good to restrict your business geographic location based up on the capability and suitable business purview. This kind of approach can restrict your competition to a good extent in order to minimize your efforts to the required extent successfully too. Here, people always go with a think big approach through keeping the geographic location as the entire world, but this kind of approach is keeping you into the huge volume competition. It is little tough to get upper hand over this kind of huge competition. So, decide your business geographic location as country wise and gain some good results. Down the line, you can expand your geographic location to the worldwide spectrum after gaining some credits from the search engine in the SEO perspective.

I am here with showing a sample page with Google keyword research tool for the search string "latest smartphones" as below:

Google AdWords										ra Cu
Home	Campaigns	Opportunities	Tools and Analysis	Billing	My account					
Keyword Planner		Your product or service								
Add ideas to your plan		Latest smartphones					Get ideas	Modify search		
Targeting		Ad group ideas	Keyword ideas				Download	Add all (38)		Your plan
United States		Ad group (by relevance)	Keywords	Avg. monthly searches	Competition	Suggested bid	Ad impr. share	Add to plan		Saved until C
All languages										
Google		Keywords like: ...	latest smartpho...	274,630	High	Rs.322.31	0%	»		Your plan is group idea o
Negative keywords		Reviews Smart...	latest smartpho...	14,760	High	Rs.382.75	0%	»		building a ne
Customize your search		Best Phone (46)	best smart pho...	50,160	Medium	Rs.497.13	0%	»		Ad groups: 0
Keyword filters		New Phone (19)	new phones, n...	33,200	High	Rs.289.69	0%	»		
Avg. monthly searches ≥ 0										
Suggested bid ≥ Rs.0.00		Smartphone Sa...	latest samsung ...	8,980	High	Rs.165.50	0%	»		
Ad impr. share ≥ 0%		Smartphone T...	top smartphon...	11,490	High	Rs.319.69	0%	»		
Keyword options		Comparison (8)	smartphone co...	7,040	High	Rs.319.85	0%	»		
Show broadly related ideas										
Hide keywords in my account		Cheap (7)	cheap smartph...	11,410	High	Rs.116.69	0%	»		
Hide keywords in my plan										

Chapter 3: On-Page Optimization

This on page optimization is the first step you will be commencing for your SEO and this should be initiated from the website development stage without fail. In fact, you can plan SEO for the existing website too, but creating some of the useful on-page optimization techniques to the existing website is little tough as it demands redesign or revamping your website very often. So, it is always good for a business website to plan their search engine optimization from the scratch and carry it forward along with the website design without fail. Currently, every small and medium business online facing huge competition and it is highly imperative to have right SEO strategies to cope up against this prevailing huge volume of competition too. My suggestion for every entrepreneur is that to have a combined strategy for the business that is through including successfully SEO practice into the daily routine. It is not tough too through having more familiarity with the practices and you can implement this dynamic strategy on own without hiring a professional too.

Our on page optimization process should be initiated from the scratch and it can be started with keeping the website design to the expectations and easy usage of the visitors. Here, this website design should ensure more usability along with the best user experience without fail. Also, it is highly imperative to create this website in HTML, Xml and less scripting codes in a way to turn into more search engine friendly as most of the search engine spiders and bots visiting your site will be having more familiarity with html, xml and simple scripting codes. Any strong or complex codes in this web design will have more chance to be ignored by the spiders and bots, when they find it hard or tough to understand too. Also, make it sure to validate all your html and xml codes using some of the online reliable tools. This kind of validation will keep your website more search engine spider and bot friendly without fail.

Also, it is quite wise to check the Google SEO guidelines before proceeding with your website design. Follow these guidelines properly in a way to accomplish compliance with these guidelines without fail too. The following links will be a great help in this context:

Google Webmaster Central Blog

Google Webmaster help Pages

Google Webmaster Guidelines

Follow the valuable information on above provided links before proceeding with your website design. It can stand into a great help to come up with the right design that is with more usability along with the best user experience without fail.

Domain Name Selection:

Domain name selection will have good command on your SEO to the reasonable extent. It is always good to have a domain name that is related to your business product or service that is matching well with the selected main keyword. Also, there is no need to be panic, when you failed to obtain such domain name for your website too. Try selecting something nearest and rest care can be taken through the meta tags submission with the Google or search engines. Select a suitable domain name and ensure all the guidelines well within the website design without fail along with creating easy navigation from page to page within the site for the visitor. Here, one more important suggestion from my point of view you are about webhosting service registration. If you have chosen a domain name that is already old and indexed with popular search engines, then no problem. If it is totally a new domain with no familiarity for the search engines, then you must gain the trust from the search engines though registering the domain for more than one year and up to five years is always a good forward step for your SEO. Here, search engines will fail to show significant attention to a new website that is registered for one year kind of short duration.

Meta Tags. Meta Title and Meta Description:

It is highly important to have meta title and meta description for the each page of your website without fail. Here, this meta title and meta description will stay within the website design and will not appear on the website. This meta description will be displayed below to the website in the web rankings. Also, this meta title and meta description offers a clear idea to the search engines about the page contents and its information. It is not a good practice from the web designer to leave this meta title and meta description field vacant. Also, website owner should create this meta title and meta description for every page from the content provider without fail and these meta title and meta description should contain the page main keyword without fail in it too. Here, it is quite imperative for the SEO professional, content writer and web designer to work together to ensure the selection of the right keywords for the website, usage of the keywords within the content and for placing the right and appropriate meta title and meta description within the design successfully.

Also, it is required to submit all the main keywords and auxiliary keywords of all pages of the website to the search engines in the field of meta tags. Generally, this will ensure the search engines to index your website in the right category within the right category based up on these meta tags, which are nothing, but the selected keywords by you for your website. Definitely, meta tags, meta title and meta description will play a vital role in the indexing procedure of the search engines. Always pay utmost attention to these aspects without fail through coordinating well the SEO professional, content writer and web designer.

SEO Content Writing:

Content writing on the website is another important on page optimization technique for the SEO. Every search engine will identify the website usability for the user based on the content and incorporated keywords in it. As I instructed earlier, select one main keyword and 4 to 5 auxiliary keywords for each page of the website using the Google AdWords Keyword planner. Use these keywords within the content from 2 to 3% without fail. Using keywords in excess can result into spamming of your website by the search engines. Also, make it sure that the content is flowing in a natural tone along with the selected keywords appropriately. There is another important thing should be remembered well while creating website content for the SEO. There is one important thing should be mentioned here. Selecting a website for the user is done through the search engine spiders and bots. These spiders and bots will view your website in the created programming language that is html or xml or some other. These spiders and bots will not view the website pages the way we does. So, there is vital point to be observed while using the keywords within the content. Never let your keyword associated with any symbols such as "?", "$", "%" and some more. Any keyword that is associated with the symbols will have a chance to understand as part of the program of the website and those will not be considered as a keyword by the spider and bot. So, keywords in the question format also should be suggested using in a sentence format through avoiding the "?" in it.

Content of the website should be rich in quality and information centric without fail though the search engine spiders and bots are not capable enough to comprehend the exact meaning of the content. Here, the content created over the website page should attract the customer base without fail. There is a chance to lose business, when content is not quality rich as your customer base will treat you as not fit for their purchase needs. Here, it is highly imperative to create this content more user friendly along with the keywords at appropriate strength.

Content creation is definitely a special on page optimization technique that can keep your site within the good web rankings successfully. This is possible only through conducting the right keyword research and through using these keywords wisely within the content without affecting the needed quality parameters. It is always good to hire a professional that is good at conducting this keyword research and creating the useful quality content for the website. Any slightest mistake at this aspect can keep your web rankings with search engine at stake. Ensure utmost precision and care at this aspect without fail while designing your website and this can result into good SEO and good web rankings for your site successfully.

Headers and Header Tags

It is always good to have headings for your website content while creating your website. Here, it is always wise to have one main heading in the form of H1 tag and two sub headings in the form of H2 tags. Also, it is quite imperative to create these headings along with the one main keyword or auxiliary keyword without fail too. This is another wise on page optimization technique for you. These headers will play a vital role in attracting the search engine spiders and bots to a great extent. When search engine spider or bot searching for keywords at your website, it is not possible to read the entire content of the page by the spiders and bots. So, these bots and spiders will try to read 1/3 part of the content and any keyword found in that process will result into indexing your page for those particular keywords.

Generally, headers are always a main priority for the spiders and bots while searching for the keywords. They will pay instant attention to these headers and added keywords in the headers will result into quick indexing of the page by the search engines. Also, there is a chance for the bots and spiders to miss some of the important keywords availability at your page as they always tend to read certain part of the content only. Here, keeping one H1 tag and 2 H2 tags with main and auxiliary keywords can result into a good on page optimization for your website besides being quick with the search engine indexing procedure to obtain the web rankings. It is always good to create your webpage in two to three paragraphs along with the suitable headings.

Image Tag Optimization

It is a very common procedure for the websites to have suitable images, logos and some more as a part of the procedure to attract the visitors and to create a brand image for the business. These images can be used wisely for your on page optimization procedure to a good extent successfully. Your website designer will create an ALT tag for these images and logos while creating HTML or xml code for the website. Use this ALT tag wisely for your SEO through naming this image with your main keyword. It is always good to name all your used images and logos on the website with the main keyword and auxiliary keywords.

I have told you earlier that search engine spiders and bots will view the web page in the programming language format unlike the way we view a web page. So, make this to your advantage through naming all your images with the keywords at the image tag area. So, when a spider or bot views this tag, then it will understand that this image is informing more about that keyword and related data. This way you're bringing more credit to your website for those keywords and your page is going to be further more SEO friendly too.

Image tag optimization through naming with keywords is a best procedure for the SEO improvement and to obtain the quick attention from the search engine too. It is always the responsibility of the website owner to insist this aspect to the good extent with the web designer. This way you can ensure another vital aspect of the on page optimization for your website through giving no scope for missing or forgetting this aspect by the website designer. Definitely, image tag optimization may sound simple, but trust me the results you will be empowering through this aspect will be enormous for sure.

Internal Links and Appropriate Strategy

Internal links are another wise approach for the on page optimization of the website. These internal links are called as bread crumbs and these will create easy navigation for the visitor as well as for the spiders and bots too. For example, you're explaining something about your product or service on the HOME page content. It is always wise to anchor link this part to the product or service page in a way the visitor can reach instantly to that page. There is nothing wrong to use this internal link strategy on every page of the website in a right way through creating this internal link through anchor linking the keyword. This kind of internal link strategy is an indication towards easy navigation all over the website and this kind usability factor will be identified well by the search engine bots and spiders in order to rate your website as more user friendly one than others. This kind of user friendly features will improve the web rankings with the search engines to a good extent too. This is the reason, why internal anchor links are regarded as the best on page optimization technique for a website.

Internal links are always a good strategy to ensure easy navigation for the visitor and there is a chance for the visitor to bookmark your site too through this kind of assurances for more usability in addition too. My suggestion is not to leave any single chance to improve your on page optimization and this anchor linking strategy can fetch you a lot in return in the form of improved web rankings for you down the line without fail.

Footer Optimization

Footer optimization is another on page optimization step for your website that can bring good results in return successfully. For example, your physical office location is in New York and you will be serving online for the entire US population. Here, create footer optimization to one or two pages of the website through creating full address along with the zip code, contact number and email. This kind of footer optimization is going to inform to all your visitors, bots and spiders that you have physical location at the New York. Also, there is a chance to serve well for the local searches to a good extent.

This footer optimization can help you well to result into an option for the local searches too. For example, a person searching for your product or service mentioning the zip code or city name, then definitely your page with this footer will be considered as the result for this user. Definitely, footer optimization is a good on page optimization technique to inform your physical location and to serve well for the local searches too. You will be benefiting in multiple ways through this footer optimization and never give a chance to miss this technique for your website. Also, this footer optimization is a best option for a website that is having multiple dealer locations at the various cities. Create a page for the each dealer in the city along with the footer and this will result into a great help for the local SEO for your website to a maximum extent successfully.

SiteMap Creation

Sitemap is definitely important aspect to improve your SEO and to ensure well quick indexing for your website with the search engines too. These sitemaps are definitely baby food for the spiders and bots. This sitemap creation will serve well for the spiders and bots through creating right idea about the entire pages of the websites and their content. It is a common practice for spiders and bots to visit the website once after submitted for indexing with the search engines. When these spiders and bots visit your site, then they look first for the sitemap in order to save time from searching the contents of the website. So, bots and spiders will always consider a website as more search engine friendly, when it is having a good site map. According to the current situation, it is always wise to create your sitemap in xml through keeping anchor linking to the each page.

Also, it is always a wise step to create this sitemap in xml along with the H1 tag. Through adding the H1 tag to each page along with anchor link, you will be informing more about the page contents with the help of the added keyword within the H1 tag. It is always good to create this sitemap keeping in mind the exact use and help for the spiders and bots in a way to turn it into more search engine friendly for sure. Many people are definitely not particular about this aspect and failing to keep the sitemap for their websites. Definitely, it is not mandatory to have a sitemap, but it is a good way to ensure quick indexing for your website from the search engines. Also, it is considered and termed as a best on page optimization procedure for a website keeping in mind the kind of value credited to the website from the search engines too.

If you're creating a sitemap, then make it sure to create it in xml and add the each page information along with the H1 tag without fail. This is definitely not tough and easy to accomplish too. Create a right sitemap and improve your SEO and web rankings with this successfully. Also, creating sitemap can result into a great help for the visitors too. A visitor will also find this sitemap as a great help, when looking for particular information from your website too.

Outbound Links Strategy

People always think that outbound links will have no value or help to their websites. But, I totally disagree with this aspect. There is a lot you can do with this outbound link strategy. We have discussed in the earlier chapters about the authority sites and the way Google identify these authority sites to keep them top in the SERP. Create an outbound link to the authority site related to your niche or to the Wikipedia kind of sites. Through this outbound link to the authority sites, you will be informing to the Google that you have sourced the content from this pioneer. There is a chance for the Google to trust your content through this approach thinking that you have been sourcing content from the right place like their way. So, make good advantage of this aspect to the good extent and add this as another important on page optimization for your website successfully.

Chapter 4-WebMaster Tools and Popular Search Engines

Web master tools are the place where you will be submitting your website for indexing from the search engines. I have provided links to the various popular search engines in my earlier chapters and there you can submit your website for indexing successfully. Previous chapter is clearly informed more about the required on page optimization procedures for the website. Complete your website in a right manner through ensuring well all the above mentioned techniques. Now, submit this completed website for indexing with your interested search engines successfully.

There will be verification process from the search engines once after submitted for the indexing. This entire verification process will take a while basing up on the prevailing competition for the chosen meta tags or keywords of the website. Definitely, a website with less competitive keywords will obtain quick indexing unlike the one with the competitive keywords. Here, keeping your website with the right on page optimization techniques will help well to a great extent to reduce this time for the indexing. This is the reason, why I completed the on page optimization chapter prior to this chapter. Also, you need to create some configuration setting here basing up on your business model and strategies. Those settings are as below:

1. **Geographic Settings**: This geographic setting is all about your business purview. You have to set your business purview according to your business strategy here in the form global, country, state, and city wise successfully. If your geographic selection is for particular location as city, then it comes under Local SEO strategy. I will be informing

more about this local SEO in detail in another chapter of this book. So, select your

business geographic location here properly.

2. **Meta Tags**: It is highly imperative to submit all your keywords of the each page

including main and auxiliary keywords in the meta tags section. Here, through providing

all your keywords in the meta tags section, you will be ensuring quick and appropriate

indexing for your website. Your created meta tags will help well to the search engine to

index your website in the right category within their database in a way the site can be

appeared right in the SERP. Many people often fail to provide these meta tags while

submitting their websites to the search engines. Always identify the real importance 0f

providing meta tags and ensure it without fail. Your provided meat tags will help well for

the search engines to index you in those keywords category in a right manner in order to

keep your website as useful for the users. Also, this is a right way to come in the SERP

and to obtain the best organic traffic for your website too. Definitely, these meta tags

provision from your side will ensure the quality organic traffic to your website without

fail. In fact, Google and other search engines normally will identify the websites though

those were not submitted with the web master tools. Sites those were identified through

this procedure will fail to get indexed in the right category as there were no meta tags

from the website owner. So, submitting on own to the web master tools will ensure right

categorization for your website and to ensure well the quality organic traffic to your

website.

Web Master Tools Features

Once after submission of the website is completed with a search engine, then regular login facility will be created through the registered email. This account will stand as an interface between your website and search engine to inform more about your site health, status, and analytics (traffic details). Mainly, you will be informed more about the crawling errors through Crawl Errors page in your Webmaster Tools dashboard. This page will inform you more about the each page status whether it is loading properly or strained through any errors. If any of your pages is facing some problems, then these details will be brought to your notice by the search engine at the Crawl Errors page demanding quick resolution to these errors.

Similarly, there is another page in your dashboard with CrawlStats and this is another important information page for you from the search engine. Google uses this page to inform, when there are any inbound or outbound link errors. For example, you're getting few or many in bound links through paid format or from a place, where the content is low or inferior in quality. These wrong practices including any red hat technology approaches will be informed to the website owner promptly at the CrawlStats page. It is always essential for the website owner to check the Crawl Stats and Crawl Errors page in order to attend quickly over the Google identified errors and mistakes. Failing to address these issues will result into spamming your website through deleting your records from the indexed database.

There is another good tool available at this dashboard in the form of Fetch Tool. This fetch tool is a great help to add any new pages of the website for the Google indexing. Generally, once after submitting the link of the new page through Fetch tool, it takes up to one week to index that particular page by the Google. Similarly, there is a facility for the website owner to block any of the website pages from crawling and indexing by the search engine. You can submit Robo.txt note pad file to the Google webmaster tools with the links of the pages those are not requiring indexing from the search engine. Google will block these pages from crawling as well as from indexing too. At one point of time, any of these blocked pages needed to be added for indexing, then delete that link in the robo.txt file and add this through the Fetch tool. So, this is clearly informing that you have privilege to block and index any of your website pages at any point of time using the robot.txt facility and Fetch tool options.

Similarly, this webmaster tools page will offer you detailed overview of the website impressions, click rate and search queries in details for you. You have to look into these details perfectly well in a way right off page optimization procedures can be planned wisely using the successful search queries in this page. Definitely, webmaster tools page of the website is a great help to identify the performance of your site in all aspects including traffic. The information provided from this dashboard is going to be a great help to plan right strategies for your SEO down the line. It is always good to plan your

SEO strategy basing up on the results taking place at your webmaster tools dashboard details.

Also, this dashboard will provide you clear overview about the present incoming links to your website along with the details about the originating source. This will give you a chance to check your link building campaign results in a right way besides others those are using your site as reference for their content needs. This links page in the dashboard will allow you to delink any of the sites that is sending inbound link to you too. This facility is mainly to offer you a chance to delink the links those are coming from wrong sites those are not belonging to your product or service category.

Webmaster tools dashboard is also place, where you will be regularly updated with the latest tools and facilities from the Google too. You can check all the Google's latest tools and facilities arranged for you and make good use of them successfully. Mainly, all these tools and facilities will be arranged to improve the usage in many ways. It is always good to keep in touch with your dashboard at regular intervals in order to learn more about your site health and performance besides availing the latest information, tools and facilities from the Google in addition.

Website performance and flaws will always be easy to learn from the Google point of view through the webmaster tool's dashboard. Especially, SEO practice basing up on the details provided at this dashboard will result into more rewarding for your website in many ways. It is always more productive to plan your SEO strategy basing up the Traffic page of the dashboard, which provides the details about the number impressions, number of clicks and successful search queries for your website. It is wise way to plan the off page optimization strategy basing up on these successful search queries in a way to target perfectly well your customer base. Definitely, there is a lot to grab trough this dashboard for you, for your website and for your website SEO too.

Chapter 5-Off Page Optimization

Off page or off site optimization is a technique that is a best option for your website's dynamic SEO. This off page optimization is a process to improve the SEO status of the website through additional choices those are completely away from the on page optimization techniques. Here, the logic is simple that on page optimization techniques are implemented only once as a permanent approach for a certain period. So, there should be an additional process for improving the site SEO through some special measures those are known as off page optimization techniques. These off page optimization procedures are designed in a way to target the ever changing interests of the markets and the customer base. As mentioned above, on page techniques are completely static with no scope to change or alter. So, some of the off page techniques are always wise option to address the changing interests of the customer base and markets in a way to turn them successfully into your regular customer base quickly. Also, keywords tend to change at regular intervals from the day website was designed and these changed keywords should be targeted through some of the off page techniques, which can turn your site as appropriate choice for these changes successfully too.

Off page optimization can be practiced successfully in multiple ways. Here, selected options will always be dependent over the site owner's interests, affordability and feasibility. Some of these approaches will require spending and some can be accomplished very easily through spending time online too. This is always essential to consider multiple options for your off page SEO as competition online is growing into enormous day by day. As long as the off page strategy is volumetric and stronger, then it will be easy to combat against your competitors online too. There is a great necessity to have dynamic SEO through keep on practicing some of the reliable off page options without fail. There is nothing wrong to consider these options at regular intervals too, when there is affordability constraint as a hurdle. Here, proper planning is always essential for a website and for their off page optimization in the form of dynamic approach or at regular intervals keeping in mind the present and future competition online for your product(s) or service(s). Plan some of the viable, suitable, feasible and appropriate strategies without fail in a way things can fall into paces successfully for the website. Definitely, off page optimization is a best process in order to stand tall online against all your competitors. Your applied on page optimization options are always a great help to keep active your business and to improve well your web rankings in order to attract he great volume of organic traffic successfully in addition too. Definitely, organic traffic obtained through the search engines is a great promise for the excellent business besides being a plus for your SEO too.

Directory Submissions:

Writing articles and submitting these articles with popular article directories along with a resource link towards your website is a well known popular off page optimization technique for many years. These are called back links or inbound links for the websites, which are always a great help to improve the SERP rankings improvements. Here, more the links, then there is a great chance to result into the top level in the SERP too. For many years, Google is regularly encouraging the quality articles written and submitted in various article directories related to your business product(s) or service(s) and considering these back links for improving your web rankings within the Search Engine Results Page (SERP) too.

There are thousands of article directories available all over the internet, but my suggestion is to go with some of the top directories those are quick at approving and publishing your articles. For example, EzineArticle directory is currently very much popular one over the internet. Here, problem is that Ezine always takes long duration to approve your article unlike other article directories and there is no guarantee that your articles will be approved and published too. Very often this directory rejects submitted articles not mentioning the exact reason. My suggestion is not to waste on these types of directories for you back links and select some of the directories like ArticleBase, which always approves and publishes your article within hours successfully. Also, my suggestion is to Google top 20 article directories and goes with few among them for your article directory submission needs. This kind of practice will help you well to obtain the quick and good results for your back link needs. Mainly, this is a genuine off page optimization technique that improves your web rankings and traffic to a great extent successfully too.

There are few things to be kept in mind while writing and submitting these articles at the directories. Always keep the keyword strength to 2% within these articles. Also, select some of the popular trending keywords related to your products or services those were not covered in your website content. This way you will be targeting additional recent keywords related to your products through article directory submissions in addition. Also, it is quite imperative for you to create authors bio of the article with your resource link and create this link in right format without fail. Any mistake in the creation of this resource link will fail to offer required results as the visitor will fail to reach your landing page. If you're totally new to this link creation, then my suggestion is to check with already published articles' resource links to follow the process properly. Here, there is one more thing to be keep in mind is that the created link should be connected to the right landing page that is very much related to the content within the article.

Social Bookmarking

Social bookmarking is another latest trend and proven results oriented off page optimization technique nowadays for every website. This social bookmarking is all about sharing your content all over the popular social networking sites those are brimming with millions of traffic related to your product and prospective customer base. Google also considers social bookmarking and resulting traffic as the quality inbound links for websites. In fact, this is not alone for improving your SEO, but also results into a great help to spread a word about your product or service to the entire world with a single click too. Definitely, social bookmarking is a best approach to project your efforts in the right format to your target customer base and markets successfully too.

Currently, there are more than 50 popular social networking sites those are suitable for your social bookmarking needs. You can manually register with all the popular sites and share your blog posts, articles and other promotional content through these accounts manually. Here, time always plays a vital role and very often people find it hard to afford required time for these needs. There are few reasonable free and paid tools available for your social bookmarking needs. My suggestion is to try one of the free tools first and successful results can keep you comfortable into a paid user down the line. Check all the available tools for this purpose and first try only free tools for acquainting more knowledge about the integrated technique in the process. This kind of familiarity will help you well to finalize a right paid tool for your requirement.

I trust and use one paid tool for this purpose, which is popular and well known all over the internet as OnlyWire. This is currently available in free and paid formats. Try this tool initially for free and basing up on the comfort levels and affordability transform into paid format later. This kind of tool will help you to spread your article or blog post to all popular social networking sites up to 50 with a single click. This will save your time and there is a great possibility to attract new customers those are into that particular product or service or information. Mainly, it is quite easy to bookmark your blog post or article or web page through this tool too. The main trick is in the selection of the right category for the sharing based on your product or service. Any website that is looking for the quick and results orienting social bookmarking can find the good solution through these tools and OnlyWire is a best option according my current experience. Social bookmarking is always good at providing valuable and rewarding results for your SEO than any other options. So, never ignore this option, when you want quick improvement to your SEO. This is very simple and easy to practice too.

Classifieds and Local Listings

Classifieds within the online classifieds site and local listings is another wise platform to inform the presence of your online business to your prospective customer base. There is little conflict with this aspect. Personally, I feel this local listings facility is a great help for a local website that is registered with Google for the local business listings SEO that is local SEO. Any global website to look for SEO improvements through classifieds and local listings is not a reality according to my opinion. Google clearly mentions that any paid or promotional activity that is with a back link will not be considered as a SEO strategy. Local listings are definitely a great help, when your website is with local SEO strategy. Also, there is nothing wrong to create ads with classifieds and local listings as this procedure is always capable enough to bring the traffic and prospective customer base towards the website continuously. It is right approach for bringing genuine traffic, but a wise option for your SEO in the form of traffic according to my personal opinion. People who still believe in this procedure for SEO can practice it successfully.

Forum Posts and Comments

All over the internet millions of the forums are available for the various categories. These forums registration and posting comments, answers and posts can result into a great help for your SEO in the form of quality back links. Here, joining into the right forums those are related to your product or service category is essential. Also, you only can post your comment or answer or post, when you are significant old with your registration. Instant registration and commenting will sound like a pure promotional activity and there is a chance for the forum to ban you thinking it as a promotional activity. Register with as many forums as possible those are all well related to business category. Keep your presence regularly at these forums and communicate well with other members. During this communication, take an opportunity to share your links as a part of the communication. This kind of approach can result into the genuine activity and genuine back links for your website. These inbound links obtained in this form from the various forums those are related to your category will add up well to your SEO and improves your web rankings to a great extent too. Generally, many people will reach various forums thinking that their questions and riddles will be answered well by the experts at the forum. So, be an expert at the forum through offering valuable information and answers to the questions and riddles along with sharing appropriate page link of your website. This is another quality off page optimization for your website, which can bring quality back links in return for your SEO improvement needs.

Blog Commenting

Blog commenting is another valuable off page optimization technique for you. It is very common practice for websites to have Web 2.0 blogs to their websites and blog posts will be published from here. Select some of these blogs those are good and regularly publishing blog posts. It is highly imperative to select these blogs from the similar category as your website without fail. Go to these blog posts and read the content properly. Every blog post normally proposes Call to Action in the form of comments from the readers. Make good use of this procedure for obtaining back links to your website. Here, you comment should be of lengthy, quality and appropriate with the content in the blog post. Post your quality comment in lengthy manner along with your website link or a link to the particular page of your website that is more relating to the blog post content. Here, comments keeping in mind with bringing back links will be spammed by the blog owner as well as Google too. Always remember that blog commenting with link can b a right approach only, when your comment is more appropriate and genuine to the blog post.

Blog post commenting is definitely a wise approach for the off page optimization requirement, but select a blog post that is matching and falling under the similar category of your business product or service. Commenting on every blog and obtaining inbound link will not serve well for your SEO as Google already mentioned in its guidelines that commenting link has to come from the similar category without fail. Definitely, it may sound simple, but definitely not. You have to keep in touch regularly with your competitors' blog posts for this purpose and write some comment from your side along with the link. Here, acceptance of this comment from the blog owner is very much essential as your comment will be available only after the approval from the blog owner (or admin). So, your comment has to be genuine, good and not damaging for this blog owner. There is a great deal of precautionary measures required for this practice besides reciprocating in the similar manner with your blog posts for others commenting. Any kind of damage acts from your side on the blog post can result into similar kind of acts from others on your blog posts too. Here, it is always essential to maintain some cordial relationship with others while planning to have some blog commenting for the back links need. Practice blog commenting and forum commenting procedure in a friendly, cordial and information providing manner in a way every one can accept it well. Blog commenting is one of the best way to demonstrate your expertise skills over the category through projecting right information and right views too. It is a better way to obtain significance for your product or service too.

Press Releases

Very regularly, I read online from the experts to publish press releases to improve the SEO. It is true that press release will offer you a chance to create valuable back links to your website, how far this can help to the SEO improvement is still at doubt. According to my opinion, press releases are always a great help to attract good volume of quality traffic towards the website, but not a help for the SEO. The back links or inbound links coming through press release will fall under promotional activity and Google guidelines always mention clearly that paid or free promotional activities will never be considered for the website search engine optimization.

Press release sites are nowadays successful in spreading the word with your present and prospective customer base. Definitely, this medium is always wise option to introduce your latest business additions with the customer base. This is a pure promotional activity like classified ads or listings. So, you can definitely expect traffic through this procedure and acquired traffic is always an additional opportunity to improve your web rankings with the search engines. But, press releases are a special approach to bring traffic and failing to improve the SEO directly as the back link received through this approach will not add to the SEO. It is a pure indirect approach, which can show significant web rankings improvements down the line. My point is that the inbound links those are coming from the press releases will not be considered as back links or inbound links for the website SEO.

Use this press release option as a genuine a way to attract the traffic and to share this press release at the social networking sites. Already, many SEO experts online confirmed this fact that press releases will not be considered for the back links. Also, you may consider or skip my opinion in this context for your website too. I always agree that a great volume of traffic will be generated successfully through the right press release. Create press releases at regular intervals and improve your web traffic at good extent successfully. This kind of improved traffic down the line can earn authority status for you with the search engines successfully. Check some of the popular press release sites and use them for publishing your press releases wisely. Traffic is always a great plus for improving the web rankings and accomplishes it successfully with the press releases.

Web 2.0 Blog

This Web 2.0 blog is currently very important and essential for every website that is looking forward to obtain good results from the off-page optimization. Add web 2.0 blog to your website and this blog page will help you well to target the trending keywords those are not covered within the on page optimization and website content. It is very well known factor that keywords will vary time to time basing up on the changing interest of the users and customer base. While creating website, the keywords used in the content will be pertaining to that period trending keywords. The keywords those are taking place as trends down the line related to your niche should be targeted wisely from your off page optimization process and your website blog pages will be a great help for this purpose too.

Write blog post regularly those are rich with your meta tags and currently trending keywords. Create an inbound link from these blog posts towards your related website pages. These inbound links are more valid to improve your SEO besides being more SEO friendly and customer friendly in many ways. This Web 2.0 blog is also called as Content Management system for your website and to create dynamic content for the website too. As mentioned earlier, the content created over the website is almost permanent until the website redesign proposal. Here, website should have a proper content management system to cover the latest trending keywords in a dynamic manner. There, you will need this web 2.0 blog as your content management system. This content management system can be carried out in WordPress, Joomla or any other technique according to the convenience.

Definitely, Web 2.0 blog is going to be a great help for your website off page optimization and to connect well with your present and prospective customer base too. Also, these blog posts will be a perfect medium for your SMM and you will have scope to share these blog posts those are with fresh content to other network members easily. These shared blog posts at the various social media networks will improve your SMM and brings organic traffic successfully. This is one way going to be beneficial for your business besides being more SEO friendly for the website in addition. Bringing in bound links from the web 2.0 blog is always easy and less technical too. A website owner also can create effective content management system through this blog with simple efforts and little learning. This blog is always a great facility to connect well with the prospective customer base those is interested in your product or service, but searching with the latest keywords.

Miscellaneous Off Page Optimization techniques

So far mentioned off page optimization practices are some of the wise and reliable approaches to improve your website SEO. In fact, above mentioned are definitely easy to implement with little efforts, but there are few more you can plan for this purpose. These are little costly approaches, but got creates good momentum to improve your business and SEO simultaneously. Those are:

- Create a mobile App related to your product or service and distribute it at free of cost to all your present and prospective customers. Also, this App sharing via SMM can improve more reliability for your business and business products too. This is little costly for developing an App, but creates very good opinion and mileage over your business products besides earning brand value in addition.
- Create an interactive widget that can be used on the current day gadgets and make this widget attractive and well connected with your business product. This will also bring similar kind of mileage like Mobile App.
- Release coupon codes for your business products or service.
- Create some contests on the internet with interesting prizes to won by the participants. This can instill good interest on the website and creates a chance for more traffic and bookmarking from the worldwide customers.
- Start donating charities and make it sure that this charity going to offer more mileage and attention to your website and business products.

- Write guest blog posts and articles for other websites those are into the similar niche.
- Create an Ebook related to your business product or service and distribute it at free of cost. This will bring good organic traffic and sales as well.
- Publish a WhitePaper on your business product or service and share with your entire customer base via social media networks, email and through other options.
- Creating own customized tool bar, creating own social media website and some more also good off page optimization techniques for your website.

Mentioned miscellaneous options are little costly and time involved options. One can plan as many options as possible as the current SMBs are strained through huge competition. This ever growing competition is easy to overcome through implementing many of the off page optimization techniques.

Chapter-6---Search Engine Marketing and paid Advertisement

Advertisements are always a best option online for the present day SMBs to gain popularity and to reach their customer base. Google PPC Ad campaign will always be the first thing in mind, whenever we talk about advertisement online. PPC ads are helping SMBs since very long, but cost involvement is always a factor that is keeping most of the businesses away from it. In this chapter, I want to explain little about the cost effective PPC ad campaigns and other advertisement options for the SMBs.

Google travelled a long way over the internet with their PPC Ad campaigns. These ad campaigns are planned using the Google Adwords keyword planner tool. This tool will offer the trending keywords related to your niche in the form of HIGH, MEDIUM and LOW status. Here, HIGH status keywords are costly affair for your ad campaign, but got good chances for the conversions. Similarly, MEDIUM status keywords are priced reasonably by Google and these keywords are helpful partly for conversions and partly for traffic improvement. Here, LOW status keywords are always my favorites. These keywords are meant to bring only traffic with less spending and chances for conversion are hard to expect.

SMBs are currently facing huge competition and during this competition business primary aim should be to bring traffic rather than to aim for conversion. If your aim is conversion and then targeted to HIGH status keywords for your ad campaign, I must tell you that are going to be in vain. This HIGH status keyword is definitely good for conversion, but customer is always more inclined towards a brand or reputed business for their purchase. So, it should be the primary aspect for every SMB to obtain popularity and reliability first rather to target conversion. Traffic is always a best option to create this reliability. Initially, use some cost effective LOW keyword that is more volume of searches every month. This will start to bring some traffic for you with very little cost involvement.

It is time to go with MEDIUM keyword after experiencing good traffic using LOW keyword ad campaign. This approach again will help you to bring traffic, few conversions and more reliability for your business. This is time now to try HIGH keyword once after obtaining reasonable popularity and familiarity with the customer base. This will result into the most effective Google PPC AdWords ad campaign approach for you. You should be careful in selecting the right keywords in this process through researching wisely with the Google AdWords keyword tool. Try this approach; you will definitely witness worthwhile results to your spending on the PPC AdWords ad campaigns.

Apart from the Google PC ad campaigns, there is some more paid advertisement channels are there with a promise for the business prosperity. Facebook paid ads comes under this category. It is quite evident that many popular brands and many small businesses currently made space within the Facebook in order to be getting connected well with their customer base. So, facebook and twitter are other promising places, where your ad can obtain huge attention successfully. In fact, ad campaigns within facebook and twitter can stand into a great support to create a brand name for the business too.

Facebook ads are currently gaining good attention and connecting well with the target customer base with very little efforts. Facebook ads are definitely hard to ignore for SMBs those are interested in gaining quick attention for their products. Also, adding an ad campaign to your social media marketing can create wonders for your business too.

Advertisement is always a cost involved aspect for every business. If your interest is for Google PPC Ad campaigns and facebook ad campaigns, then suggested regularly checking for offers and discounts from these two pioneers. Definitely, some of these offers can help you well to reduce the financial burden involved in your ad campaigns.

Advertisement content is another vital aspect while planning to have ad campaigns. Already, these advertisements medium is very much familiar to all SMBs. It is indicating once again competition for your ad campaigns. Here, different kind of ad campaign that is completely away from the routine path is essential. It is always important to observe your competitors ad campaign while planning yours. Create something innovative, attractive and completely away from others. Nowadays, customers are also fed up with the regular ads and no longer falling for these ad campaigns unless there is something enticing within the ad content. Create your ads those are matching well to the better interest of the customers.

Regularly we see many ads with regular content those are rich with target keyword. You should make little different on this aspect. Currently, customers knew it well that their interested product is available everywhere or at multiple places. At this point, every customer is more intrigued about the price factor. Make this as an advantage for creating your ad content. Keep your ad content with discount offers and price economy. Definitely, this will lure the customer base to the good extent and they will tend to click over the ad without fail. This kind of approach and planning will turn your advertisement strategy more viable and effective for your business.

Chapter-7 Social Media Marketing

Currently, SEO strategies for small and medium business are mainly dependent over three special components and those are Links, Content and Social Media. This is clearly indication, how important is your social media marketing plan to improve your business as well as SEO. The world digital marketing is hard to complete without involving the social media effectively into it. The power of present day social media is enormous and to extent got ability to influence over the customer base too. If you want to compete against your business competitors wisely, then it is essential to have proper social media marketing strategy. This SMM refers to a process that is capable enough to bring traffic to the website in a way the traffic can convert into sales from the popular social media networking sites. Your business message or product information can be made familiar to the entire customers in this world through using wisely available popular social media networks. Your message not only heard by the people and it will resonate successfully all over the world through this approach too. There is another beneficial aspect involved in this marketing approach too and that is its cost effective nature.

SMM creates a chance for the proper leveraging of your powerful content and helps well to connect with the worldwide customers instantly. Here, it is quite imperative to have proper understanding and familiarity about the social networking site working and features without fail. Otherwise, the planned entire strategy may turn into in vain and often result into fatal for the business too. There are few fundamentals to be given utmost importance while implementing your SMM. Those fundamentals are:

- SMM marketing is all about sending more messages from the business in a way there will be more chance for listening than talking. This is indicating that you should provide valuable content for your audience in a way they will read it with attention rather than to come up with quizzing. For this, you should understand well your target customer base interests at social media networks. You can obtain this kind of grip over the target audience through observing and reading their shared contents and their responses towards that information. This kind of observation will offer you a great level of familiarity about the interests of the target customer base at the various social networks. So, create your content in a way that can match well to these audience and they will definitely pay attention to it.

- Your initial step at and strategy with SMM should be focused over building a brand rather than targeting conversions or sales. Here, your customized content and other strategies will help well to create a brand for your products at the social media networks successfully.

- Quality should always be a paramount interest for your SMM rather than quantity. It is always better to have some of the best connections in limited numbers within your network those are matching well to your business product strategies. This kind of approach will bring prospective results for your business. It is not good to have too many connections as at one point or other people with varied interest will result into damage for the developed popularity within the social networks and this is definitely not a good sign for the successful SMM plan.

- Patience should always be an integral strategy of your SMM plan. It is not possible to obtain overnight success with SMM. People at the social network sites are always choosy and they will take more time to observe and to select you as their source of buying. So, watch your step and word always in a better way with patience as an integral part of it.

- Your successful presence with best approach at the various social networking sites like Facebook, Twitter, LinkedIn and some more will definitely offer a lot in return. When you started sharing some of the interesting content topics at these places, people will start to share it with their friends. This kind of activity will result into compounding positive results for your business as well as for your SEO too.

- Your constant appearance at the various social networking sites through the SMM plan can result into influencing over the audience down the line. You should act properly to create this influence. Make it sure to bring some of your existing customers into the network and create interesting communication with existing customers in a way the customers can feel like getting more attention and concern from the seller. This kind of attention paid by the business towards the existing customers will create more reliability for your products and business. The prospective customers within the network will instantly fall for this and tend to turn into customer eventually.

- Your presence shouldn't be a dedicated approach at the social networking sites as this will result into negligence from others. You should create your presence at specific timings and make it sure that your presence felt by others through paying attention and concern on others. This will make them to wait for your arrival and this is a good sign to create an impression on others wisely.

- There should be proper acknowledgement system from your side towards other network members. You should regularly accept, appreciate and share others content without fail.

This will create a good relationship and friendship environment among all and they too will start to reciprocate the same for your content too.

- It is highly essentially for you to keep your presence once after publishing and sharing your content at the social networking sites. If you disappear instantly, then people will think that content is not up to the standard.

- Above all, it is highly imperative to be friendly with all including those are trying damage your image on these networking sites. Your cool answers and composed nature with these bullying people will add into a better addition in building your popularity. If you ignore other people negative comments, then it will tend to be true. So, please be attentive and responsive with positives and negatives with similar friendly approach.

Chapter 8 Visual Content Ideas

Gone are the days with your SEO strategy and planning. People are keeping away from the monotonous practices and looking for something novice. Your regular content ideas require taking special paths for this purpose and these novice approaches can help you well to keep your business above ahead over your competitors too. People are nowadays more into visual content rather than textual content. Some of the valuable visual content ideas you can be planned wisely with your SEO strategy are Graphics, Videos and PowerPoint presentations.

Graphics and Graphical Content: There are many graphics based social networking sites currently resulting into special approach for the SMM. Some of those are Instagram, Pinterest, Flickr and some more. Do you know that these graphics sharing sites are nowadays helping a lot to build your brand too? Create some brand logo, images of your products with rich graphical representation. Publish these graphical representations at the popular graphical content promoting social networking sites as mentioned above. People those are found to be interesting your images will have a chance to like or pin them. These Pins and likes are again add up well to your SEO in an enormous way and these are another perfect white hat approach to bring valuable inbound links to your site too. If you find it as a costly affair to hire a graphics expert for this purpose, then try some free graphics creation tools online. Initially, usage of these tools may be little tough, but down the line things will start to fall into places successfully.

Videos: Definitely, there is no necessity to inform much about videos at present. All your videos related to your product or business can bring more mileage and attention instantly. Mainly, these videos are nowadays obtaining huge volume of attention from the worldwide public too. Use this interest wisely for your SEO improvements. Create more videos in enticing format and publish them at YouTube, Vimeo and some more popular video sharing network sites. Here, proper optimization is necessary for your video. While publishing your video at the various sites, make it sure to create keyword rich video description along with a keyword rich title and list tags. Create some WhiteBoard videos on your product along with SEO friendly title and description and those will instantly reach to the prospective buyers through search engines and through sharing these videos at the popular social networking sites like Facebook and Twitter too. This approach will keep your videos in the search page rankings quite easily and in turn will add up well to your SEO too.

PowerPoint Presentation: PowerPoint presentation is another kind of visual content approach for your SEO. Currently, many people regularly visiting www.slideshare.com for these presentations. These presentations will also bring similar mileage like videos. Create your product WhitePaper in the form of PowerPoint presentation and publish it at the mentioned site. Here, too create a SEO friendly title and description for your presentation along with tags. This way you can connect this presentation to your prospective buyers those are searching via search engine. Also, you can share these presentations at the social networking sites too and you will be surprised for the kind of attention those will obtain from the network members. In fact, creation of powerpoint presentation is nowadays very easy and can be completed on own with little efforts too. It is indicating that, it will require no spending in addition for this approach.

Chapter 9- Local SEO

SEO is definitely major integral part of the digital marketing for SMBs. Here, it is highly imperative to consider your local SEO in a special way keeping in mind the latest trends and search engine practices. As public are nowadays more into browsing internet through the various gadgets, search engines are offering more perfection towards their local search results. Search engines like Google, Yahoo and Bing are taking more precautions about the validity of their local search page results too. It is clear indication, how important it is to have a special approach for the local SEO with the current day competition enriched SMBs. This is the reason, why separate special chapter is dedicated in this book to handle this topic in a special way.

It is pretty common nowadays for SMBs to have website, but SEO should be prioritized for this purpose basing up on the target customer base. So far mentioned SEO practices in the previous chapters of the book are perfect for the global or country wise SEO strategies. Here, when a business target customer base and business services are particularly for a segment or location or a city, then local SEO practices should practice in a special way. First of all, while submitting your website for the various search engines' web master tools, mention the geographic location as that city or place. This kind of particular geographic location selection is called local SEO. All the search engines are emphasizing special measures towards the websites those are local. Especially, people very commonly look for their interested product or service details availability online through their smartphones and tablets. The results obtained through local SEO needs to be more realistic for this purpose. For keeping these search page results for locals, search engines are practicing more verification approaches for the reliability. So, SMBs those are targeting local customers alone should have special approach and special SEO strategies without fail.

Websites submitted for local SEO require following few special steps. While submitting your site for the local SEO, create some description of your business or products or service along with the keywords within 250 characters. Also, add suitable and appropriates tags for this purpose. You have to provide your business address and contact number without fail. Here, every business should be more careful in providing these details. Make it sure you will provide the verifiable address and a phone number that is having more chances to be working all the time. Search engines like Google will send a post card to this address for verifying its address and status. Down the line sometimes there will be a phone call to the registered phone number in order to find out whether the business is active or not. This verification process is mainly to ensure that the business is available in live for the searchers. During this verification process, the businesses those are with not working phone numbers will be verified through the activity of the business's official social media accounts at Facebook, Twitter and some more. Also, this verification will be extended up to gathering feedbacks at the popular listing sites, classifieds and some more too. Any business that is found to be not traceable through verification will be temporarily removed from the indexing until there is a response from the business entity.

Local SEO definitely require special measures unlike global SEO in the form of proving their live activity through all means such as phone, social media presence and some more. Also, it is quite imperative for these local businesses to emphasize more over local listing sites and directories like Yelp, Yellow Pages, Local and some more and try to obtain some feedback at these places from your customers at regular intervals, These feedback scores obtained will result into good inbound links for your local SEO besides being authoritative verification for the business activity in addition too. Also, posting regular ads and classifieds on the popular listings and classified sites online can cater well to the SEO and help well to retain the good search page ranks for the business too. Here, major difference is classifieds as these classifieds will not be of any help for global or country SEO of the website, but works well for the local SEO.

Local SEO has to be considered in a special way and here categorizing, selection of keywords, creation of SEO friendly business description, emphasizing more on local listings are vital aspects shouldn't be missed at any cost buy the small and medium business entity. People often consider local SEO as very simple activity, but it is not. There is a lot to be exercised in it through the mentioned aspects.

There is something more should be mentioned in this local SEO section. Most of the franchisees like pizza delivery points, hotels, ice cream parlors and some more should take more precaution about their content. When a franchisee is creating a local website, make it sure not to use the content from the franchisor's website. It will be counted as copied content by the search engine. Though you are selling the same product from the franchisor, create your own unique content for your website without fail.

Similarly, a business having main office in a city and having multiple dealers in other cities should play carefully here. This business is suggested having additional pages for each city dealer with product details within their main website along with local address footer optimization. This will help well, when a person looking locally for your product. Also, it is a good idea to have different local websites for the each dealer too. My suggestion is to create a separate site for each dealer in the various cities. This way, the product can be easily in reach for a buyer that is searching for it locally on the search engine.

Definitely, franchisees and dealers will require local SEO for targeting their local customer base. It is always ideal to have special separate digital marketing approach that is totally away from the franchisor or main business. This way, a business can reach well to their customer base successfully. Local SEO is definitely a special format and implement it wisely through fulfilling all the requirements of the search engines at the same time emphasizing more on the local listing and social media marketing.

Chapter 10 – Digital Marketing Step by Step

Below, I created a check list for your digital marketing that can be followed in a step by step manner for your business:

- Domain name selection is the first step in the process. Select a domain name that is informing more about your business product and matching well with the high trending keyword. Definitely, keyword in URL can result into a great help for the SEO, but not mandatory too.

- Create meta title for every website page using the page main keyword once and using once any of the secondary keyword.

- Create meta description for each page using once main keyword an secondary keyword of the page and this description should be kept up to 250 characters.

- Keyword density in your webpage is another important aspect while creating content. It should be wise, when you kept this keyword usage up to 3%.

- Keep your content easy to understand and do not uses much jargon. Also, ry to have H1 and H2 tags in your content and create these headings using keywords wisely in a way the spiders and bots can see them clearly.

- Search engine spiders and bots cannot read images within the website pages. I is suggested naming the image alt tag with the page main keyword, which can result into gaining good attention from the spiders and bots in a way to improve your SEO.

- Select one main keyword and 4 to 5 secondary keywords for the each website page. Use these keywords wisely within the content.

- Create some bread crumbs within the each page content in a way the visitor can have easy navigation from page to page. Here, bread crumbs are nothing, but anchor link s in the page content that can transport he visitor to other page of the website through a single click.

- Also, create some outbound link s to the authority sites like Wikipedia or some other of your niche. It will inform to the search engine spiders and bots that website creation followed and sourced valuable information from the authority sites. This will add more value to your site from the search engines.

- Try to get some inbound links from the blogs, article directories, res releases, social media marketing and some more. Here, never let this inbound link is coming for the similar IP address or C Class of the website. Such inbound links will turn into neutral and gain no value for your SEO.

- Apply some paid advertisement strategies like Facebook ads, Google AdWords ad campaigns and some more.

- Practice valuable social media marketing.

- Practice some of the viable visual content ideas.

Some Technical Tips:

- When Java Script used for image maps, dropdown menus, image links, then make it sure to keep text links in a way spiders can follow the script very easily.

- There will be a problem while using Ajax, frames and Flash for the website through not letting it to link with a single page. Here, suggestion is not to use frames and use AJAX and Flash sparingly.

- Always enable "Enhanced Image Search" option within your Google Webmaster Central Account and this will obtain good attention for your SEO.

- Always try to select a web hosting service provider that is having hosting server nearest to the target customer base. If this hosting server is far away from the customer base, then it will take very long time to load your website for the visitor.

www.ingramcontent.com/pod-product-compliance
Lightning Source LLC
Chambersburg PA
CBHW021441170526
45164CB00001B/340